FUNGI POWER

FUNGI as FUEL AND OTHER PRODUCTS

Cherry Lake Press
Ann Arbor, Michigan

by Joyce Markovics

CHERRY LAKE PRESS

Published in the United States of America by
Cherry Lake Publishing Group
Ann Arbor, Michigan
www.cherrylakepublishing.com

Reading Adviser: Beth Walker Gambro, MS, Ed., Reading Consultant, Yorkville, IL

Content Adviser: David S. Hibbett, PhD, Clark University, Worcester, Massachusetts

Book Designer: Ed Morgan
Book Developer: Bowerbird Books

Photo Credits: © Ed Morgan, cover, title page, and table of contents; © freepik.com, 4–5; CDC/Wikimedia Commons, 6; © freepik.com, 7; © Tintila Corina/Shutterstock, 8; © luchschenF/Shutterstock, 9; © Tintila Corina/Shutterstock, 10–11; © KYTan/Shutterstock, 12; © freepik.com, 13, 14; © imageBROKER/Gerald Abele/Newscom, 15; © freepik.com, 16; © Y.P.photo/Shutterstock, 17; © Loop Biotech. All rights reserved., 18, 19; © Ecovative/Ferrari/ZUMA Press/Newscom, 20–21; © freepik.com, 22–23; © kharisma yogik/Shutterstock, 24; © freepik.com, 25, 26–27, 26 bottom, 28, 29 top and bottom.

Cherry Lake Press is an imprint of Cherry Lake Publishing Group.

Library of Congress Cataloging-in-Publication Data has been filed and is available at catalog.loc.gov

Printed in the United States of America

CONTENTS

FUTURE FUEL

An airplane zooms across the sky. It leaves a trail of exhaust. Seconds later, the plane disappears behind a cloud. Jet fuel powers this and other aircraft. Fuel also makes energy to light up our homes and run our cars. Many of the fuels we use come from plants and **algae** (singular alga) that lived and died millions of years ago. Over time, heat and pressure turned these once-living things into oil, coal, and natural gas. These are called fossil fuels.

To create energy, people burn fossil fuels. But there's a cost. Burning fuel pollutes the environment. Harmful **pollutants** are released into the water and air. One such pollutant is carbon dioxide. Once in the air, carbon dioxide acts like a blanket that traps heat in the **atmosphere**. As a result, the planet warms, leading to climate change. Climate change causes the weather to become more extreme. It affects how much rain falls. Climate change also causes sea ice to melt and sea levels to rise. And Earth becomes a harsher place for many living things.

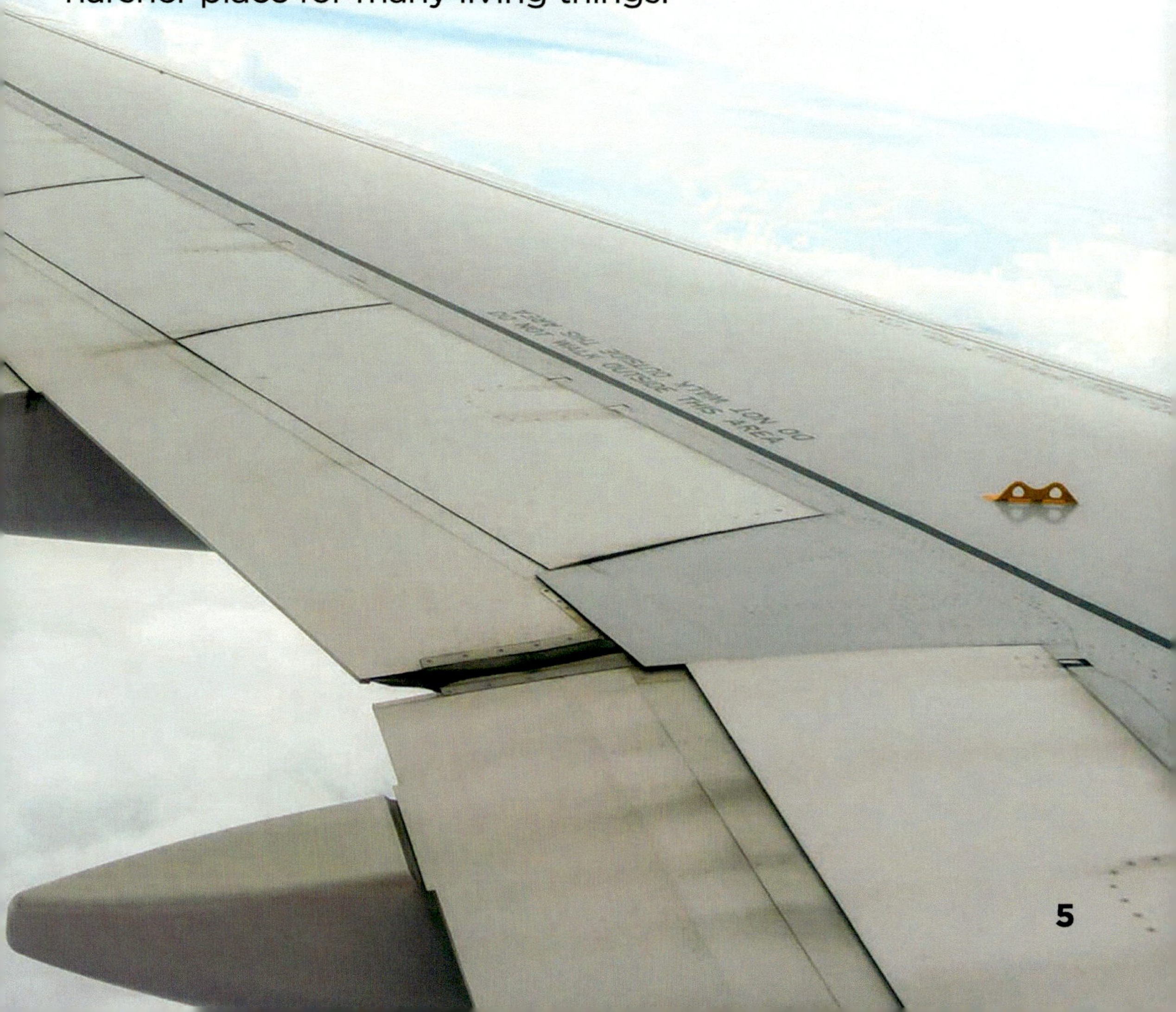

Thankfully, there are **alternatives** to fossil fuels. Some are made using incredible organisms called fungi (singular fungus). For example, a common black fungus can make jet fuel! The fungus is found in old leaves and soil. Amazingly, it produces hydrocarbons, a central **component** of oil and natural gas. Scientist Birgitte Ahring studies the fungus. "It produces a blend that is pretty similar to what you have in a normal jet fuel," Birgitte said. She thinks the fungus produces hydrocarbons to protect itself from certain **bacteria**.

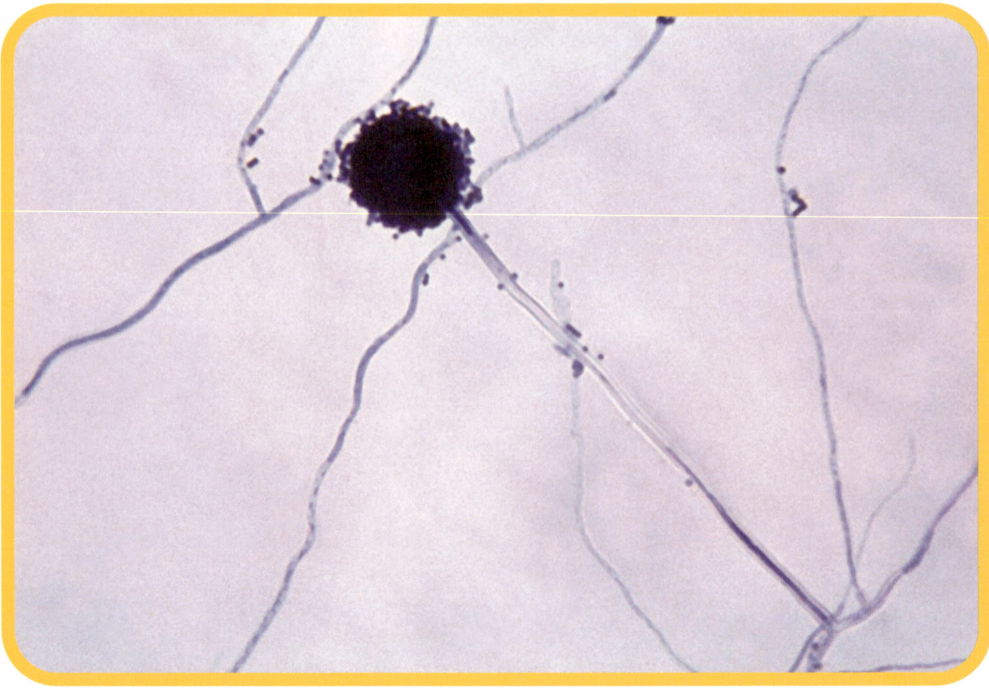

The black fungus is called *Aspergillus carbonarius*. It's a type of mold. Here's a sample of an *Aspergillus* fungus under a microscope.

Making jet fuel in this way has many pluses. It's simpler than processing fossil fuels. "Fungi also have the great potential to make fuel at a low cost," said Birgitte. In addition, the fuel creates less carbon dioxide. But it's not easy to make large amounts of the hydrocarbons. Birgitte and her team are still working on increasing productivity. "It's very promising," Birgitte said. "It's a tremendous opportunity."

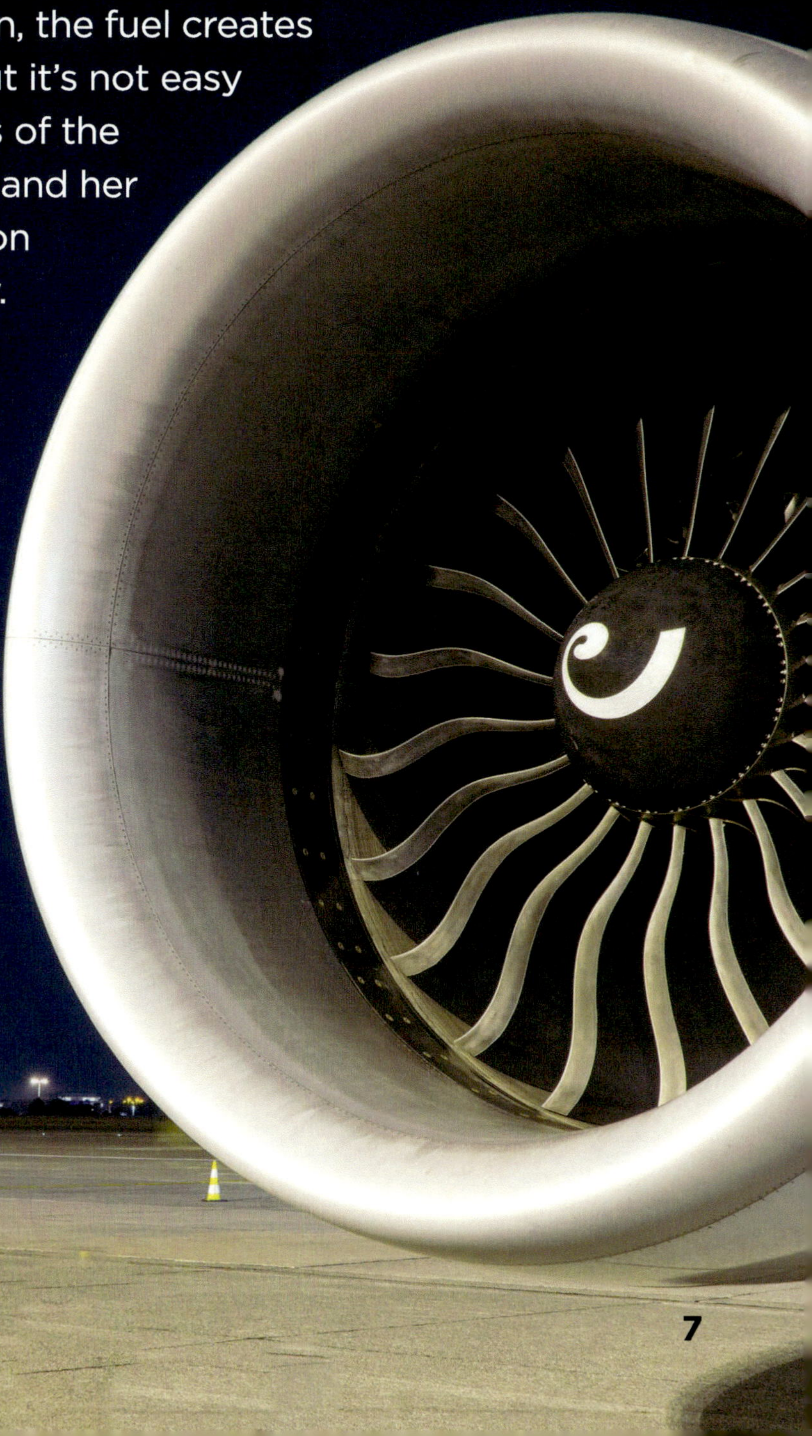

To power their engines, airplanes need fuel—lots of it.

Fungi can produce fuel in other ways, too. The fungus *Trichoderma reesei* breaks down plant material. It was first discovered during World War II (1939–1945). Soldiers found that it rotted their cotton tents and uniforms. In 2013, researchers combined the fungus with bacteria. They put both organisms in a tub filled with dried corn stalks. First, the fungus went to work, creating **enzymes**. These chemicals broke down the stalks into sugars. Then the bacteria transformed the sugars into isobutanol (eye-soh-BYOO-tuhn-awl), a colorless fuel. It can power cars and other machines. In the future, it could replace gasoline entirely!

The fungus *Trichoderma* growing on wood

Other researchers are using fungi to make fuel cells. Like batteries, fuel cells **generate** electricity. "We have combined two types of fungi to create a functioning fuel cell," said scientist Carolina Reyes. The fuel cell is made with a 3D printer. Fungi and **nutrients** are added to the **resin**. Then the printer forms the resin into a grid. As the fungi **digest** the nutrients, they make electricity. Now, Carolina and her team are working on making the fuel cell more powerful.

This is an example of a typical fuel cell. The fungi fuel cell is nontoxic and can break down naturally.

FUNGI Facts

Biofuels are made from living things such as fungi. These fuels are renewable because they can be replenished.

A Cool Kingdom

Fungi aren't just used to make fuel and fuel cells. They can be made into hundreds of different things! The products include everything from packing materials and **acoustic** panels to lamps and coffins. Fungi are fascinating. But what do you really know about them? When you hear the word *fungus*, do you think of mushrooms growing on a log? Or maybe you think of foot fungus. *Yuck*!

Fungi include a vast variety of life. There are 160,000 known kinds of fungi. Sometimes, fungi are mistaken for plants. But they're very different. Experts say they are more similar to animals. The truth is fungi make up their own special kingdom. Fungi range from mushrooms and molds to yeasts and mildews. Some are microscopic. One kind is the largest organism on Earth! Fungi live almost everywhere, even on **glaciers**, in deserts, and on the seafloor.

Armillaria ostoyae is also called the honey mushroom.

FUNGI Facts

Known as the humongous fungus, *Armillaria ostoyae* is the largest known living thing on Earth. It lives mostly underground in Oregon, covering nearly 4 square miles (10 square kilometers)!

Fungi surround us. But we can't see most of them. That's because many are microscopic and the places where they thrive are mostly hidden. But if we were to dig in the dirt, we would find miles of tiny white threads. These threads, called hyphae (HAHY-fey), belong to fungi. As hyphae grow, they form clumps that look like cotton candy. This weblike mass is known as mycelium (mahy-SEE-lee-uhm). It is the body of fungi. And it has an important job—to find food.

Mycelium in the soil

Unlike plants, fungi can't make their own food. So, using their hyphae, they thread their way through the soil in search of a meal. Fungi "eat" a lot of dead stuff. When they find something tasty, they release enzymes. These chemicals dissolve their food. Then the fungi take in the nutrients they need. But some also share nutrients and water with plants. In return, the plants pass on sugars to the fungi through their roots.

A type of fungus called a morel mushroom grows in a forest. It has a large underground network of mycelium.

FUNGI Facts

Fungi and plants rely on each other for survival. This relationship helps keep ecosystems healthy.

Mushrooms are the visible parts of certain fungi. When conditions are just right, they appear. Mushrooms are the so-called fruiting bodies of fungi. Fruits of plants contain seeds. However, fungi contain something different—spores. A spore can grow into a new fungus. Mushrooms have gills, which are bladelike structures under their caps. The purpose of the gills is to make spores. After being released, the spores are transported by the wind, water, or animals. This helps them find a new place to grow.

These are the gills on the underside of a mushroom.

Some fungi don't have gills. They release their spores in other ways. For example, the hedgehog mushroom has tiny toothlike parts that hold its spores. The giant puffball shoots its spores out through a hole on its top. Once airborne, the small spores look like a cloud of smoke. Coral fungi have colorful branching parts. They are covered in a fine spore-containing layer. When the spores mature, they shoot out. Now that you know the basics, let's explore some more products made from fungi!

Above is a hedgehog mushroom with its spiky underside.

Eco-Friendly Things

Fungi are being used to create a lot of useful things. In many cases, products made from fungi could replace **traditional** materials one day. One example is packing material. For decades, Styrofoam has been used to package everything from food to glass. But Styrofoam is toxic. It contains many harmful chemicals. And it is not **biodegradable** or recyclable.

However, there is a solution involving fungi! A company called Evocative is making "mushroom packaging." It's made by growing mycelium on farm waste, such as corn stalks or wood chips. The material is grown in molds and then dried. It offers the same packing protection as Styrofoam. Yet it's fully biodegradable. After it's used, the mushroom material can be **composted**. In just months, it breaks down.

Packaging made from mycelium next to mushrooms

FUNGI Facts

Enough Styrofoam is produced each year to circle the Earth. Styrofoam fills up a lot of the space in landfills. Mycelium packaging could help change this!

Fungi can also be used to grow coffins! Many people are embalmed after they die. Their bodies are filled with chemicals to disinfect and preserve their remains. But the chemicals are harmful. They can seep into and pollute the ground. Also, people cut down trees to make wooden coffins. Is there an eco-friendlier way to bury the dead?

This mycelium coffin is called the Loop Living Cocoon™

Mushroom coffins enrich the Earth, not pollute it.

A company called The Loop Biotech came up with an idea. "In the forest, we found our answer in mycelium . . . nature's most powerful recycler," said the company's founders. So, they made a living coffin from fungi. First, mycelium is mixed with wood chips. Then it's grown in a coffin-shaped frame. Once the mycelium has filled the frame, the coffin is dried. This stops the mycelium from growing. When the coffin is fully dried, it is strong enough to hold a human body. After the body is placed in the coffin, water is sprayed on it. This can cause the mycelium to start growing again. Then the process of **decomposition** begins.

Loop also makes a mushroom urn called the EarthRise™ to hold a person's ashes.

FUNGI Facts

The mycelium coffins are grown using local mushrooms in only 7 days. They fully decompose in 45 days.

Outside of coffins, fungi are being made into other things, including lighting. Danielle Trofe is a designer who focuses on **sustainability**. "I grow lamps from mushroom mycelium," said Danielle. "It's basically nature's glue." She uses waste from crops to nourish the mycelium. Then she makes molds in the shape of lights. To make an individual lamp, Danielle hand presses the mixture into a mold. In 4 to 5 days, the mycelium finishes growing. Finally, she bakes the lamp.

Here is one of Danielle's lamp designs.

People have jokingly asked Danielle, "Can I eat the lamp?" "Yes, you could, but it would not taste good," she replied with a giggle. "But that's exactly what we're trying to achieve here," Danielle said. "Something so natural that you could eat it." She calls her lights MushLume. One of her goals is to encourage people to think about the materials they use. "And get us a little more connected to our things," said Danielle. For her, the future of fungi is bright.

FUNGI Facts

Mycelium products are lightweight. They're also fire- and moisture-resistant.

MORE USES

Some people call scientist Timothy Hsu a "fun guy." Why? He's using mycelium to change the world of acoustics. Acoustics is the science of sound. When acoustics are good, sounds are clear and easy to hear. Products called sound panels help improve acoustics. "One of the most common types of panels is this foam, fuzzy stuff you see on the walls," said Timothy. They prevent echoes and create quieter spaces. But they can be harmful to the environment. So, Timothy came up with a solution: mycelium sound panels.

The process for creating the panels is similar to making coffins and lamps. After the mycelium panels are grown and baked, Timothy tests them. They're hung in a small room. Sometimes, he plays the piano in the space. This helps Timothy decide how well the panels work. In the future, he imagines acoustic art made from mycelium. What else can mycelium be made into?

Good acoustics are essential when hearing live music.

Scientist Athanassia Athanassiou has an answer. She also makes things from fungi. She focuses on materials that can biodegrade and replace plastic. One area of interest is bandages. She uses mycelium to develop a product that's like **gauze**. But it also helps wounds heal! "When you have an open wound and then you put the **fibrous** material on it, this slowly gives the wound the time to self-heal," said Athanassia.

Mycelium growing in bags

FUNGI Facts

A company called Mogu produces mycelium flooring tiles. They're as long-lasting as stone. But they're more comfortable to walk on.

One day, mycelium bandages could replace traditional ones.

Athanassia also discovered how to alter the stiffness of her mycelium products. The harder the substance the mycelium is grown in, the stiffer the mycelium. For example, wood chips make mycelium more rigid. Potato peelings, on the other hand, grow softer material.

Athanassia is looking into other uses for these products, such as in the field of **robotics**. "These biodegradable materials . . . they are very flexible, so they can be used for robotic skins." She hopes to build a completely biodegradable robot one day.

for the environment. However, making fungal products on a large scale is challenging. But scientists and creators are hard at work. Every day, they are making advances. They see endless possibilities for fungi. "There are thousands upon thousands of species of fungi," said David Hibbett, a **mycologist**. "We're just starting to explore a few of them for making materials."

FUNGI Facts

A fungus is even being used to make houses for bees! Fungal extracts may also help bees fight off certain viruses. But more research is needed.

WHO KNEW?
FUN-gi Facts

Orchid Friends

Orchids produce some of nature's most beautiful flowers. Yet without fungi, they might not exist. The partnership starts when orchids are seeds. In order to **germinate**, fungi must enter the seeds. As they grow, young orchid plants get most of their nutrients from fungi. In exchange, the fungi get food and water. This is known as a symbiotic (sim-bee-OT-ik) relationship.

Fungi as Foe

Most fungi are good guys. However, some attack plants and animals. For example, one type of fungus kills banana plants. It prevents water from reaching the plant's leaves. Another fungus feeds on the skin of live bats. Called white-nose syndrome (WNS), it has caused millions of bat deaths. An even deadlier fungus is thought to have wiped out an entire species of toads in Costa Rica!

Lichens

You've probably seen a patch of crusty lichens (LYE-kuhnz) clinging to a rock. But did you know that lichens are made up of two living things—a fungus and an alga? They live so closely together that they look like one organism. The fungus provides a home and water for the alga. And the alga uses the sun's light to make food for the fungus. Because of this teamwork, lichens can live in extreme places, like deserts.

GLOSSARY

acoustic (uh-KOO-stik) relating to how well sound can be carried or heard in a room

algae (AL-jee) tiny plantlike living things that grow in water

alternatives (awl-TUR-nuh-tivs) a choice of one or more possibilities

atmosphere (AT-muhs-fihr) the mixture of gases surrounding Earth

bacteria (bak-TIHR-ee-uh) tiny life-forms that can be seen only under a microscope

biodegradable (bye-oh-dih-GRAY-duh-buhl) able to be broken down naturally

component (kuhm-POH-nuhnt) a part of something

composted (KAHM-pohst-uhd) made into compost, natural material that has rotted

decomposition (dee-kahm-puh-ZISH-uhn) the process of something rotting or breaking down into another form

digest (dye-JEST) to break down food

ecosystems (EE-koh-siss-tuhmz) communities of animals and plants that depend on one another to live

enzymes (EN-zahymz) substances that cause chemical reactions, such as digestion

fibrous (FAHY-bruhs) containing or consisting of threads

gauze (GAWZ) a very thin fabric that is used to cover wounds

generate (JEN-ur-ayt) to produce

germinate (JUR-muh-nayt) to begin to grow or develop

glaciers (GLAY-shurz) huge, slow-moving masses of ice

mycologist (mahy-KAHL-uh-jist) a person who studies fungi

nutrients (NOO-tree-uhnts) substances needed by fungi and other living things to grow and be healthy

pollutants (puh-LOOT-uhnts) harmful substances that contaminate the land, water, or air

resin (REZ-in) a thick, sticky liquid

robotics (roh-BAHT-iks) the study of robots

sustainability (suh-STAYN-uh-bill-uh-tee) a way of living that does not use up natural resources

traditional (truh-DISH-uh-nuhl) long-established

viruses (VYE-ruhss-iz) tiny germs that can invade cells and cause diseases

LEARN MORE

BOOKS

Boddy, Lynne. *Humongous Fungus*. New York: DK, 2021.

Bonkoski, Ariel. *Mushrooms & Fungi for Kids*. New York: Adventure Publications, 2025.

Gravel, Elise. *The Mushroom Fan Club*. Montreal, Canada: Drawn and Quarterly, 2018.

Plants & Fungi. New York: DK, 2023.

WEBSITES

Explore these online sources with an adult:

BBC World Service: Surprising Things You Can Make with Mushrooms
Fungi Foundation: Fungi Education
Kew Gardens: Secret Fungi in Everyday Life Kids Britannica: Fungus
PBS Learning Media: Fungi

INDEX

ABOUT THE AUTHOR

Joyce Markovics has written hundreds of books for kids. She lives in an old house along the Hudson River. Joyce is fascinated by fungi and what we don't yet know about these extraordinary life-forms. She would like to dedicate this book to Ed, a fungi-tastic designer, partner, and friend, and express gratitude to mycologist David Hibbett for his expertise and generosity in creating this book.